AF528533

Preface

The field of Database Management Systems (DBMS) is a cornerstone of modern information technology, playing a critical role in how data is stored, managed, and retrieved in today's data-driven world. As organizations across the globe increasingly rely on efficient data management to drive their operations, the demand for skilled professionals in DBMS continues to grow. Recognizing the significance of this field, the Indira Gandhi National Open University (IGNOU) has incorporated Database Management Systems as a key component of its curriculum, challenging students to master both the theoretical frameworks and practical skills necessary to excel in this domain.

This book, IGNOU Database Management Systems Previous Years Unsolved Papers (MCS-207), is a thoughtfully compiled collection of unsolved question papers from previous years. It is designed to serve as an indispensable resource for students preparing for their exams in DBMS. The primary aim of this book is to equip students with a comprehensive tool to self-assess their understanding, pinpoint areas that require further study, and enhance their problem-solving capabilities.

We believe that practicing with previous years' question papers is one of the most effective strategies for exam preparation. It not only familiarizes students with the types and formats of questions they may encounter but also deepens their grasp of the subject matter by applying concepts to practical, real-world scenarios. By working through these unsolved papers, students will be able to evaluate their readiness, improve their time management skills during exams, and build the confidence needed to tackle complex questions.

The choice to leave the papers unsolved is intentional. We encourage students to engage actively with the material, think critically, and explore various approaches to solving the problems presented. This method promotes independent learning and ensures that students are well-prepared to adapt to the diverse question formats and difficulties they may face during the actual exams.

This book covers a broad spectrum of topics within Database Management Systems, including relational database design, SQL, transaction management, normalisation, and data security. Each paper has been carefully selected to provide comprehensive coverage of the syllabus, offering students a thorough understanding of the core concepts essential for success in their exams.

We hope that this book will not only support students in their academic pursuits but also inspire them to delve deeper into the field of Database Management Systems. As technology continues to evolve, the knowledge and skills gained in DBMS will be instrumental in shaping the future of data management and information systems.

We would like to extend our sincere thanks to the IGNOU faculty and students who contributed to the development of this book. Your feedback and insights have been invaluable in ensuring that this book meets the needs of today's learners.

I wish you success in your studies and your future endeavours in the field of database management systems.

Table of Contents

MCS-207

Post Graduate Diploma in Computer Application (PGDCA)
Chapter 1: Term-End Examination, December, 2021
MCS-207: Database Management Systems

Time: 3 Hours
Maximum Marks: 100
Weightage: 70
Note: (i) Question No. 1 is compulsory.
(ii) Answer any three Questions from the rest.

1. (a) A university is planning to maintain the following details :
i. A unique student identification.
ii. Name of the student.
iii. Programme code in which student has enrolled.
iv. Programme names of all the programmes.
v. Programme duration.
vi. Programme fee.
vii. The contact phone number of the student.
viii. The fee paid by the student along with date of payment.

Perform the following tasks for the description given above:
(i) List all the entities, as per the description. 2
(ii) List all the attributes of the entities, as per the description. 2
(iii) Relationship between/among the entities of the description given. 2
(iv) Draw an ER diagram, as per the description given. 2
(v) List all the constraints-including primary and foreign keys. 2
(vi) Convert the E-R diagram to relations. 2

(b) Write SQL commands for the queries on the following relations: 8
Account (account-number, name, balance) Bank (branch-code, account-number, phone)
(i) List all the account numbers in the order of "name".
(ii) Find the account-number, which has the highest balance.
(iii) List the branch-code, account-number, name and balance of each account.
(iv) Find the number of accounts in each branch.

(c) Explain the term transaction in the context of database management system, with the help of an example. What are the problems associated when concurrent transactions are executed? Explain any ***one*** of these problems with the help of an example. 10

(d) Explain the relational model of database management system. Also, differentiate between a relational database management system and an object-oriented database management system. 8

(e) Define the first normal form in the context of relational database management system. 2

2. (a) List and explain any ***six*** advantages of database management system. 6

(b) What is the use of an index in RDBMS? If two indexes were created in a database– one on primary key and other on secondary key, which of these two indexes will be of more advantage? Justify you answer with the help of an example. 6

(c) What is SQL? Explain the create table command of SQL with the help of an example. 4

(d) Explain the one-to-one and many-to-many relationship in ER-diagram. 4

3. (a) What is lossless join decomposition of a relation? Explain with the help of an example. 6

(b) Explain the three level DBMS architecture with the help of a diagram. How does the three-level architecture relate to date independence? Explain with the help of an example. 8

(c) Explain the second normal form and third normal form with the help of an example of relations. 6

4. (a) What is Data Recovery? How can it be performed? Explain with the help of an example. 6

(b) Explain the term query optimisation in the context of a DBMS with the help of an example. 6

(c) Consider the relation R = {A, B, C, D, E} and the set of functional dependencies
(i) What is key in R? 3
(ii) Decompose R into 2NF and 3NF. 5

5. Explain the following with the help of an example/diagram, if needed : 20
(a) Data Mining
(b) Data Warehousing
(c) NoSQL databases
(d) Locking in transaction
(e) Weak entity

MCS-207

Post Graduate Diploma in Computer Application (PGDCA)
Chapter 2: Term-End Examination, June, 2022
MCS-207: Database Management Systems

Time: 3 Hours
Maximum Marks: 100
Weightage: 70

Note: (i) Question No. 1 is compulsory.
(ii) Answer any three Questions from the rest.

1. (a) Consider the following proposed system for a bank.
"A bank wants to store the following information of its customers using a database management system:
i. Details of customer, where each customer is given a unique identifier. The bank stores the customer name, address and contact phone.
ii. The details of every account, where each account number is unique. In addition, the bank holds the account balance, type of account (like savings account or current account) and the customer identifier of the customers who own that account.
iii. An account may be a joint account of more than one customer. In addition, a customer can own many accounts.

Perform the following tasks for the description of the bank given above: 12
(i) List all the entities, as per the description.
(ii) List the attributes of the entities.
(iii) List all the relationships between entities.
(iv) List all the constraints including primary and foreign keys.
(v) Draw an ERD for the above.
(vi) Convert the ERD into relations.

(b) Consider the following relations:
Student (enrol_no, name, course_code)
Course (course_code, title, duration)
Write SQL commands for the following queries: 8

(i) Find the course_code and title of those courses, whose duration is more than one month.
(ii) List the title of the course taken by the student, whose enrol_no is 'S01'.
(iii) Count the number of all the courses.
(iv) List the enrol_no, name, title, duration for all the students.

(c) What are the problems of concurrent transactions? Explain with the help of an example of each. 9

(d) Explain the terms Data Mining and Data Warehousing. How is data warehousing related to database management system? 8

(e) Explain the concept of referential integrity with the help of an example. 3

2. (a) Consider the relation:
R = {A, B, C, D, E, F}
and the set of functional dependencies
(i) What is the key of R? 3
(ii) Decompose R into second normal form and third normal form. 5

(b) What is the meaning of dependency preserving and lossless decomposition? Explain with the help of an example of each. 8

(c) What are the four properties of transactions in a database management system? 4

3. (a) What are the three levels of database architecture? Explain the purpose of each level with the help of a diagram/example. 6

(b) Explain using an example, how logs of a database system can be used for database recovery. Also define the concept of recovery in a database system. 7

(c) Explain the features of object-oriented database management system. How is object-oriented database management system different from relational database management system? 7

4. (a) What is meant by the term ''Query Optimisation''? Explain with the help of an example. How is query optimisation different from query evaluation? 7

(b) Explain the concept of physical data independence and logical data independence with the help of an example of each. 6

(c) Explain the concept of locking in RDBMS. How does locking solve the problems of concurrent transactions? Explain with the help of an example. 7

5. Explain the following terms with the help of an example : 5*4=20
(a) Join Operation
(b) Weak Entity
(c) Primary and Secondary Index
(d) Deadlock
(e) Database Security

Post Graduate Diploma in Computer Application (PGDCA)
Chapter 3: Term-End Examination, December, 2022
MCS-207: Database Management Systems

Time: 3 Hours
Maximum Marks: 100
Weightage: 70

Note: (i) Question No. 1 is compulsory.
(ii) Answer any three Questions from the rest.

1. (a) A bank maintains the following information about its customers :
i. A unique customer identifier
ii. Name of the customer
iii. Account numbers of the customer (a customer can open many accounts)
iv. Balance in each account with the bank
v. The phone number and address of the customer
vi. The withdrawals or deposits made in different accounts.

Perform the following tasks for the description given above:
(i) List all the entities. 2
(ii) List the attributes of the entities. 2
(iii) Identify relationships between/among the entities. 2
(iv) Draw E-R diagram. 2
(v) Convert E-R diagram to relations. 2
(vi) List all the constraints, including primary and foreign keys. 2

(b) Consider the following relations:
Student (id, name, phone, p_code)
Programme (p_code, title, duration, credits)
p_code is programme code.

Write the SQL commands for the following queries on the two relations given above : 4*2=8
(i) List the id and name of all the students of Programme, whose p_code is "MCA".
(ii) Find the programmes which have more than 80 credits.
(iii) Find the number of students in each programme.
(iv) List id, name, p_code, title of all the students of the programme whose p_code is "CIT".

(c) Explain the following terms in the context of DBMS, with the help of an example for each : 10

(i) Transaction
(ii) Locking
(iii) Checkpoint

(iv) Recovery
(v) Query cost

(d) Differentiate between the following: 8
(i) Relational database management systems and object-oriented database management systems
(ii) Data Mining and Data Warehousing

(e) What is an update anomaly? Explain with the help of an example. 2

2. (a) Explain the concept of data independence, with the help of an example. 4

(b) Explain the concept of super key, candidate key and primary key in a relational database system, with the help of an example. 6

(c) Explain the concept of generalization and specialization in the context of E-R model, with the help of an example. 5

(d) What are primary index and secondary index? Which of them is more advantageous? Explain with the help of an example for each. 5

3. (a) Given the following relational schema:
Student (student_id, name, coursecode, coursename, marks)
with the following constraints:
i. The student_id is unique for each student.
ii. Coursecode is unique for each course.
iii. A student can take many courses.
iv. The marks of a student in a particular course are recorded in marks attribute.

Perform the following tasks for the description given above:
(i) List all the functional dependencies, in the relation. 4
(ii) What are the anomalies in the relation above? Explain. 6
(iii) Normalize the relation into 2NF and then 3NF. 5

(b) Explain the term multi-valued dependency, with the help of an example. 5

4. (a) Explain ACID properties of a transaction with the help of an example. 6

(b) Explain the log-based recovery technique, with the help of an example. 8

(c) What is a natural join operation? Explain any one algorithm that can be used to implement join operation in a RDBMS. 6

5. (a) Explain the following in the context of object oriented and object relational database management systems:

2+2+4=8

(i) Complex data types

(ii) Type inheritance
(iii) Object definition language

(b) Explain the concept of multi-dimensional data in data warehouse, with the help of an example. 6

(c) Explain the concept of classification and clustering in the context of data mining. 6

Chapter 4: Most Asked Important Questions Part-A

Q.1. Describe the architecture of a traditional RDBMS.

Answer: A traditional RDBMS architecture comprises three layers internal, conceptual, and external commonly called the three-level ANSI/SPARC model. The internal level handles physical storage, defining how data is stored on disk, access paths (indexes), and file structures. The conceptual level is the global database view: the logical schema that describes all entities, relationships, and integrity constraints without physical details. The external level consists of multiple user views or subschemas, tailored for various application functions or users (e.g., accounting view, HR view). Each external view accesses data through the conceptual schema, which in turn maps to the physical storage. This abstraction ensures data independence: logical changes in the conceptual schema don't affect application views, and physical changes don't affect the conceptual design. The DBMS engine manages request parsing, optimization, execution, transaction, and concurrency control. Query processor parses SQL queries, optimizes them via the plan generator, and executes them using the storage manager. Transaction manager ensures ACID properties and coordinates with recovery manager for fault tolerance. This layered architecture simplifies schema design, improves maintainability, and ensures stable, multi-user access.

Q.2. Explain Data Independence and its types.

Answer: Data Independence allows changes in one schema level without impacting other levels. There are two primary kinds: Physical and Logical. Physical Data Independence means changes to internal storage file structures, indexing strategies, or record placements—don't affect the conceptual or external schemas. For instance, converting from heap file storage to B+ tree indexing should not require modifying application queries. This independence shields developers from low-level optimizations. Logical Data Independence means changes in the conceptual schema like adding new entities, attributes, or relationships don't affect existing external views and applications, as long as dependencies are managed. For example, adding an optional "email" attribute to a "Student" table doesn't break existing queries. Achieving logical independence requires layered view mappings and well-designed views that avoid embedding hard-coded structures. Logical independence tends to be more challenging to maintain because external applications often implicitly rely on specific table designs. Proper use of views, abstraction layers, and careful mapping between schemas preserves data integrity and eases evolving application requirements without disruptive code changes.

Q.3. Define Functional Dependency and give examples.

Answer: A Functional Dependency (FD) is a constraint between two attribute sets, expressed as X → Y, meaning if two rows share the same X values, they must have the same Y values in a relation. For example, in a Student(StudentID, Name, DOB, DeptID) table, StudentID → Name,DOB,DeptID holds because a StudentID uniquely identifies all other attributes. In a CourseAssignment(StudentID, CourseID, Instructor) table, the composite key StudentID,CourseID → Instructor means the pair uniquely determines who teaches the course. Functional dependencies underpin relational normalization: they help identify redundancy and anomalies. They form the basis for defining keys and normal forms: a candidate key is a minimal attribute set X such that X → all other attributes, and primary key is one chosen from candidates. Partial dependencies, where a subsystem of a composite key defines non-key attributes, violate 2NF. Transitive dependencies, where X → Y and Y → Z indirectly imply X → Z, violate 3NF. Identifying all FDs in a relation is essential for normalization, schema design, and enforcing data integrity.

Q.4. Write short note on Armstrong's axioms and closure of attribute sets.

Answer: Armstrong's axioms are sound and complete rules to infer all functional dependencies from a given set:

1. **Reflexivity**: If Y ⊆ X then X → Y. Any superclass functionally determines its subclass.
2. **Augmentation**: If X → Y then XZ → YZ. Adding common attributes to both sides preserves the FD.
3. **Transitivity**: If X → Y and Y → Z then X → Z. A chain of dependencies can be combined.

From these, further rules derive, such as Union, Decomposition, and Pseudo-transitivity. These axioms define the closure F^+: the set of all FDs implied by a given FD set F. We compute the attribute closure X^+ to determine all attributes functionally dependent on X. To find keys, compute X^+ and check if it contains all relation attributes; if minimal, X is a candidate key. For normalization, Armstrong's axioms guide identifying lossless decompositions and verifying dependency preservation. Automated tools use these principles to validate designs. These axioms provide both a theoretical foundation and practical mechanism for ensuring relational schemas maintain consistency, integrity, and non-redundancy.

Q.5. Explain partial and transitive dependencies with examples.

Answer: A partial dependency occurs in relations with composite keys when a non-key attribute depends on part of the key. For instance, in Enrollment(StudentID, CourseID, StudentName, Grade) where the composite key is (StudentID, CourseID), StudentName depends solely on StudentID—a part of the key. This violates Second Normal Form (2NF). The remedy is splitting into Student(StudentID, StudentName) and Enrollment(StudentID, CourseID, Grade) to eliminate the partial dependency.

A transitive dependency is when a non-key attribute depends on another non-key attribute, which depends on the primary key. Example: Book(BookID, Title, AuthorID, AuthorName). BookID → AuthorID (direct), AuthorID → AuthorName. Thus, AuthorName depends transitively on BookID, violating Third Normal Form (3NF). We fix this by separating: Author(AuthorID, AuthorName) and Book(BookID, Title, AuthorID).

Partial dependencies cause redundancy in composite-key tables, while transitive dependencies cause indirect redundancy. Both can lead to anomalies: update, insertion, and deletion anomalies. By decomposing tables to meet 2NF and 3NF, we ensure each non-key attribute depends directly and only on the key, eliminating unintended side-effects and improving data integrity.

Q.6. Discuss different types of keys in a relational relation.

Answer: Relational schemas use varied key types to uniquely identify and link data:

1. **Superkey**: Any attribute set whose values uniquely identify tuples.
2. **Candidate key**: Minimal superkey—no attribute can be removed without losing uniqueness.
3. **Primary key**: One candidate key selected to enforce entity integrity.
4. **Alternate key**: Candidate keys that are not chosen as the primary key.
5. **Composite key**: Candidate key composed of more than one attribute.
6. **Foreign key**: Attribute(s) in one relation referring to the primary key of another, enforcing referential integrity.
7. **Minimal key**: Often synonymous with candidate key, emphasizing minimality.

8. **Surrogate key**: Artificial key (e.g. auto-incremented number), not derived from domain data.

Primary keys enforce uniqueness and not-null constraints, ensuring each record is distinguishable. Foreign keys maintain relational consistency across tables. Choosing between natural vs surrogate keys impacts portability and privacy. Proper key design supports indexing, efficient querying, and normalization, all essential for robust database systems.

Q.7. Explain various normal forms up to 5NF with practical examples.

Answer: Normalization rules lead to progressively refined table structures:

1. **1NF**: Atomic values only—no repeating groups.

   Example: Split multi-valued "PhoneNumbers" into separate rows.

2. **2NF**: Achieve 1NF and remove partial dependencies:

   Example: Enrollment(StudentID, CourseID, InstructorName) → separate Instructor table.

3. **3NF**: Eliminate transitive dependencies:

   Example: Book(BookID, AuthorID, AuthorName) → separate Author table.

4. **BCNF**: Strengthen 3NF; every determinant must be a candidate key.

   Example: If Lecturer→Course and Course→Department, but Lecturer isn't key, decompose further.

5. **4NF**: Removes multi-valued dependencies:

   Example: Freight(FreightID, Product, Carrier) where Product and Carrier vary independently—split into two tables.

6. **5NF**: Also called Project-Join Normal Form. Addresses cases where data reconstructs only by joining more than two tables:

   Example: Sale(ProductID, StoreID, TimeID) each combination valid but no direct FD binds pairs—requires three separate tables to cover all possible joins without redundancy.

Advancing through these forms ensures minimal redundancy, removes anomalies, and improves maintainability.

Q.8. What is denormalization? When and why is it used?

Answer: Denormalization is the deliberate addition of redundancy into a normalized schema to optimize query performance, especially in read-heavy systems. Highly normalized structures (3NF, BCNF) often involve many joins, which are costly at scale. To reduce join operations, denormalization consolidates tables—e.g. adding aggregate columns like total_sales in an Order table. Another approach involves storing derived attributes, duplicating reference data (e.g. AuthorName in Book), or merging lookup tables into entity tables. While this improves query speed and simplifies access patterns, it introduces update anomalies, inconsistency risk, and increases storage. Therefore, denormalization is justified when performance gains outweigh maintenance costs—common in online analytical processing (OLAP), data warehouses, and large-scale reporting systems. Strict controls, triggers, or application logic often guard against anomalies. In modern distributed databases (like NoSQL), denormalization is frequently built-in for scalability. The key is striking a balance: maintain data integrity while enabling efficient, large-scale data access.

Q.9. Define ER-model. Describe its basic constructs.

Answer: The Entity-Relationship (ER) model is a conceptual data modeling method that represents real-world domains in terms of entities, relationships, and their attributes. Core constructs:

1. **Entity**: A real-world object with independent existence, such as Person, Product, or Course. Represented as rectangles.
2. **Attribute**: Property or characteristic of an entity or relationship. Includes simple, composite, derived, multi-valued, and key attributes; depicted as ovals.
3. **Relationship**: Associations between entities: unary, binary, or ternary. Represented as diamonds connecting entity rectangles.
4. **Cardinality constraints**: Specify numeric relationships (1:1, 1:N, M:N), e.g. each Student enrolls in many Courses.
5. **Participation constraints**: Whether all instances must participate in the relationship (total vs partial).
6. **Weak entity**: Cannot be uniquely identified by its own attributes. Dependent on a strong entity via identifying relationship and symbolized with double borders.
7. **Identifying relationship**: Connects weak entities to owner entities.

ER modeling visually captures data requirements, serving as a blueprint for database design. The model supports schema documentation, stakeholder communication, and logical mapping to relational schemas, enabling normalization and implementation planning.

Q.10. Explain mapping cardinality in ER diagrams.

Answer: Mapping cardinality specifies how many instances of one entity relate to instances of another in ER relationships. The common patterns are:

1. **One-to-One (1:1)**: Each instance in both entities maps to exactly one counterpart. Example: each Employee has one ParkingSpot. Rare and often simplified by merging tables.
2. **One-to-Many (1:N)**: One entity instance associates with multiple instances in the other, but not vice versa. Example: A Department has many Employees, but each Employee works for one Department.
3. **Many-to-One (N:1)**: The reverse of 1:N; semantically the same, based on perspective.
4. **Many-to-Many (M:N)**: Multiple instances across both entities correspond. Example: Students enroll in many Courses, and each Course has many Students. In relational mapping, M:N is implemented via a junction (associative) table linking primary keys.

Cardinality constraints guide relational schema mapping: they determine where foreign keys go (in N-side for 1:N) or if an associative entity is needed for M:N. They also influence database normalization and help enforce referential constraints in the actual implementation.

Q.11. What is specialization/generalization in ER modeling? Give examples.

Answer: Generalization and Specialization represent inheritance in ER modeling:

1. Specialization is a top-down process where a generic entity (superclass) is divided into one or more sub-entities (subclasses) based on distinguishing features. Example: Person specializes into Student and Faculty both inherit common attributes (Name, DOB) but have unique ones (Major for Student, ResearchArea for Faculty).
2. Generalization is bottom-up combining similar entities into a broader superclass. For instance, merging UndergradStudent and PostgradStudent into a unified Student with specific attributes segregated in subclasses can consolidate design.

Key concepts include:

1. **Disjointness constraint:** Determines if subclasses are mutually exclusive (disjoint) or overlapping.

2. **Total vs partial participation:** Indicates whether all superclass entities must belong to a subclass (total) or not (partial).

3. **Attribute inheritance:** Subclasses inherit superclass attributes.

Mapping these to relational tables can follow single table (all fields in one), table per subclass, or table per hierarchy strategies, each balancing redundancy, null handling, and query efficiency.

Q.12. Define weak entity with an ER example and its relational mapping.

Answer: A weak entity lacks a unique primary key on its own and depends on a strong/owner entity for identification. It is denoted by a double rectangle in ER diagrams and connects via a double diamond identifying relationship. Example: Dependent (on employee) with attributes (DepName, DOB, Relationship) is weak because there could be multiple Dependents with the same DepName under different Employees. It cannot exist without a specific Employee.

Relational mapping involves:

1. Employee(EmployeeID PK, Name, Dept)
2. Dependent(EmployeeID PK, DepName PK, DOB, Relationship)

Here, Dependent uses a composite primary key: (EmployeeID, DepName), referencing EmployeeID as a foreign key. The identifying relationship becomes a foreign key constraint with cascade rules. This mapping enforces referential integrity—Dependents can't exist without a valid Employee and preserves the weak entity's dependency semantics.

Q.13. Distinguish inner join, left/right outer join, and full outer join with examples.

Answer: These SQL joins combine rows from two tables based on matching conditions, handling unmatched records differently:

1. INNER JOIN returns rows where there are matching values in both tables. Example: SELECT S.*, E.Sal FROM Student S INNER JOIN Enrollment E ON S.ID = E.StudentID; fetches only students with enrollment records—unmatched entries are excluded.

2. LEFT OUTER JOIN (or LEFT JOIN) returns all rows from the left table, plus matched rows from the right. Unmatched right side returns NULLs. Example: SELECT D.Name,

E.Name FROM Department D LEFT JOIN Employee E ON D.DeptID = E.DeptID; returns every department, including those without employees.

3. RIGHT OUTER JOIN is similar but returns all rows from the right table. Example: get all employees including those without departments.

4. FULL OUTER JOIN returns all rows when there's a match in either table, filling missing counterparts with NULL. Example: SELECT S.ID, E.CourseID FROM Student S FULL OUTER JOIN Enrollment E ON S.ID = E.StudentID;—shows all students and enrollment records regardless of matching.

These join variants help express different data retrieval needs—filtering, preservation, inclusion of null records depending on report requirements.

Q.14. Explain the concept of views in SQL. How are they used?

Answer: A view is a virtual table derived from a SQL query over one or more base tables. It abstracts complex queries, simplifies data access, and enforces security. When you create a view using CREATE VIEW ViewName AS SELECT ..., the DBMS stores only the query definition—not the data executing it at runtime unless the view is materialized. Views offer:

1. **Security**: Limit column or row access (e.g. CREATE VIEW HR_Employee AS SELECT Name, Dept FROM Employee;).
2. **Simplicity**: Encapsulate complex joins or aggregations, enabling reusable abstraction.
3. **Consistency**: Provide a stable schema interface even if underlying tables change.

Updatable views allow INSERT, UPDATE, DELETE operations directly, but only if they meet specific criteria—no joins, aggregates, DISTINCT, or groupings. Materialized views store precomputed results, boosting performance for heavy queries but needing refresh strategies for data consistency. In advanced systems, views help implement logical data independence, hide schema complexity, and support modular application development while enhancing maintainability and enforcing security.

Q.15. What are indexes? Explain B+ tree and hash indexes.

Answer:

Indexes are auxiliary data structures that improve data retrieval performance by enabling faster search, insert, and sort operations. Two common types:

1. B+ Tree Index: A balanced tree structure with all values in leaf nodes, which are linked sequentially. Internal nodes store key values to guide search. B+ trees efficiently handle range queries (e.g., BETWEEN), prefix searches, and support insertions/deletions with logarithmic time complexity. Widely used in enterprise DBMSs for its versatility.

2. Hash Index: Uses a hash table where each key maps to a bucket via a hash function. Ideal for equality searches (e.g., =, IN), but poor for range queries. Hash indexes offer constant-time lookup on average, but performance degrades with collisions unless managed carefully.

Both index types improve SELECT speed but incur overhead: slower INSERT/UPDATE/DELETE due to extra maintenance, and increased storage. They also affect physical design: clustered indexes determine data file order; non-clustered indexes maintain separate structures referencing data rows. Optimal indexing requires balancing read/write workloads, query patterns, and storage constraints.

Q.16. Describe the query execution process in RDBMS.

Answer:

The RDBMS query execution pipeline involves several key stages:

1. Parsing: SQL statements pass through a parser that validates syntax and semantics. It generates a **parse tree** based on query grammar.

2. Validation & Semantic Analysis: The query processor verifies table names, column names, data types, and integrity constraints. If valid, it converts the syntax tree into a logical query plan.

3. Optimization:

a. Logical optimization, like rewriting queries using heuristics (e.g., predicate pushdown) to reduce intermediate data size.

b. Physical optimization, where the optimizer selects specific **operators, indexes**, and **join algorithms** (nested-loops, hash joins, sort-merge).

c. Cost-based optimization estimates I/O costs, CPU, and memory to choose the most efficient plan.

4. Plan Generation: The finalized **execution plan** is a tree of operators ready for execution.

5. **Execution**: The **execution engine** traverses the plan, performing operations such as scans, joins, filters, and aggregations. It reads data from disk (using buffer management) and processes tuples accordingly.

6. **Result Return**: Output is returned to the client/application, either as a result set or confirmation.

Understanding this process helps optimize queries, create efficient indexes, and reduce bottlenecks by addressing parsing errors, plan suboptimality, or inefficient operator choices.

Q.17. Compare nested loops join, hash join, and sort-merge join.

Answer:

These are common join algorithms used in relational DBMSs:

1. **Nested Loops Join**: For each row in the outer table, scan the inner table to find matching rows. Simple and works well for small tables or when one table is indexed on join keys. Efficient for small datasets but suboptimal (O(N×M)) for large tables.

2. **Hash Join**: Two-phase process—**build** a hash table on the join key of the smaller table, then **probe** it with rows from the larger table. Achieves O(N+M) time complexity. Ideal for equality joins, but requires memory for the hash table and can degrade into simpler algorithms if memory is insufficient.

3. **Sort-Merge Join**: Sorts both tables on join keys, then performs a merge similar to merge sort. Efficient for pre-sorted or disk-based data; good for range joins and large datasets. Time complexity is O(N log N + M log M), favoring sorted inputs or external sorting systems.

The optimizer selects among them based on table sizes, existing order (indexes), join type, and memory availability. Each has trade-offs in CPU, I/O, and memory usage, so selection depends on workload and data distribution.

Q.18. Explain functional dependency preservation in decomposition.

Answer:

Dependency preservation ensures that after decomposing a relation into smaller relations, all original functional dependencies (FDs) can still be enforced through constraints on the decomposed relations, without requiring expensive joins. Suppose relation R with attributes {A,

B, C} has FDs A → B and B → C. If we decompose R into R1(A, B) and R2(B, C), both dependencies are preserved because A → B applies to R1 and B → C applies to R2.

Preserving FDs is essential for integrity: if a dependency is lost, enforcing it requires joining back the decomposed tables, leading to performance hits and complex constraint management. While **lossless-join decomposition** ensures no data is lost or spurious when rebuilding the original relation, **dependency preservation** ensures we can maintain constraints on each fragment independently. There are cases (like BCNF decomposition) where dependency preservation conflicts with losslessness; the usual compromise is to achieve **3NF**, allowing both properties to hold. Designers must weigh these factors, especially in high-assurance systems where integrity enforcement is crucial.

Q.19. What is a lossless-join decomposition? Explain conditions.

Answer:

A **lossless-join decomposition** ensures that decomposed relations can be joined to reconstruct the original relation without introducing spurious tuples. Given R(X) decomposed into R1(Y) and R2(Z), the join is lossless if **Y ∩ Z → Y** or **Y ∩ Z → Z** holds. In practical terms:

1. If the intersection of attributes between R1 and R2 is a **key in at least one** of them, the decomposition is lossless.
2. Often validated using the **chase algorithm**, which simulates join dependencies.

For example, in R(A, B, C), if we decompose into R1(A, B) and R2(A, C), and A is a key in both or at least R1, then decomposition is lossless because A → B or A → C holds. Without meeting this condition, join may add extra rows, corrupting data. Ensuring losslessness is critical during normalization because correct decomposition should avoid redundancy without compromising data integrity. It provides the foundation for safe schema refinement.

Q.20. Explain relational algebra and list its operators.

Answer:

Relational algebra is a formal procedural query language foundational to relational DB systems. It defines operations that take relations as inputs and produce relations as outputs. Key operators include:

1. **Selection (σ)**: Filters rows based on a predicate (e.g., σ Age > 18 (Student)).

2. Projection (π): Selects specific columns and removes duplicates (e.g., π Name, DOB (Student)).

3. Cartesian Product (×): Combines each row of one relation with every row of another.

4. Union (∪), Intersection (∩), Set Difference (−): Set-based operations on relations with compatible schemas.

5. Rename (ρ): Renames a relation or its columns for clarity or compatibility.

6. Join: Combines related rows from two relations—**theta join**, **equijoin**, **natural join**.

7. Division (÷): Returns rows in one relation matching all entries in another.

Derived operators include **aggregate functions** and **aggregate with grouping**, though these are extensions. Unlike SQL, relational algebra is procedural—users specify how to obtain a result. It's used in query optimization, providing a theoretical foundation for rewrite rules and cost estimation.

Q.21. Describe tuple relational calculus and domain relational calculus.

Answer:

Both are **declarative, non-procedural** relational query languages founded on predicate logic:

1. Tuple Relational Calculus (TRC): Uses tuple variables referring to entire tuples. Example: { t | Student(t) ∧ t.Age > 18 ∧ t.Department = 'CS' } defines the set of Student tuples where age > 18 and department is CS.

2. Domain Relational Calculus (DRC): Uses domain variables representing attribute values. Example: { <sId, sName> | ∃a (Student(sId, sName, a) ∧ a > 18 ∧ sName LIKE 'A%') }.

Both language optimisers express **what** to fetch, not **how**, leaving execution strategy to the DBMS. They form the theoretical basis for SQL and relational completeness, proving any algebraic query can be expressed via calculus. However, TRC and DRC can be **unsafe**—queries may yield infinite or unintended results if not constrained properly. To ensure safety, domain restrictions or schema-based limiting predicates are enforced. While not used directly in applications, they underpin query optimization and foundational theory in database curriculum.

Q.22. Compare relational algebra and relational calculus.

Answer:

Relational Algebra and **Relational Calculus** are foundational formal query languages with distinct characteristics:

1. **Nature**: Algebra is **procedural**, instructing "how" to retrieve data via operations. Calculus is **declarative**, describing "what" to retrieve without specifying execution methods.

2. **Operators vs predicates**: Algebra uses explicit operations (selection, join, projection), while calculus uses logical predicates and quantifiers to define result sets.

3. **Execution**: Algebra aligns closely with DBMS internal execution plans. Calculus requires query rewriting into algebraic form for execution.

4. **Expressiveness**: Both are **relationally complete**, meaning they can express the same range of queries, though forms differ. Extensions add aggregate operators.

5. **Safety and readability**: Algebra avoids risks of unsafe queries, while calculus can yield unintended infinite results if not properly constrained. Algebra's explicit semantics may be easier for optimization.

6. **Usage**: Algebra forms the basis of SQL's internal machinery. Calculus informs SQL's predicate logic foundation.

Understanding both enhances comprehension of query planning, logical query transformation, and database theory, enabling more effective schema design and optimization strategies.

Q.22. What are the different types of SQL subqueries? Explain with examples.

Answer:

SQL subqueries are queries embedded within another query to produce intermediate results that the outer query uses. They can be categorized into single-row and multi-row subqueries, correlated and non-correlated subqueries, and scalar subqueries. A single-row subquery returns only one row, such as finding employees earning more than the average salary: SELECT Name FROM Employee WHERE Salary > (SELECT AVG(Salary) FROM Employee);. A multi-row subquery returns multiple rows and uses operators like IN, ANY, or ALL, for example, SELECT Name FROM Employee WHERE DeptID IN (SELECT DeptID FROM Department WHERE Location='Delhi');. A correlated subquery depends on the outer query for its execution and is evaluated for each row of the outer query, as in SELECT Name FROM Employee E WHERE Salary > (SELECT AVG(Salary) FROM Employee WHERE DeptID = E.DeptID);. Scalar subqueries return a single value and can be used wherever a constant is allowed. These subqueries help simplify complex queries but may impact performance if not optimized carefully.

Q.23. Differentiate between correlated and non-correlated subqueries.

Answer:

Correlated subqueries are executed repeatedly, once for each row of the outer query, because they refer to columns of the outer query within their WHERE clause. For example, SELECT Name FROM Employee E WHERE Salary > (SELECT AVG(Salary) FROM Employee WHERE DeptID = E.DeptID); requires evaluating the inner query separately for each employee to compute the average salary of their department. Non-correlated subqueries, on the other hand, run only once and their result is reused by the outer query. For instance, SELECT Name FROM Employee WHERE Salary > (SELECT AVG(Salary) FROM Employee); calculates the average salary once and then compares all employees' salaries to it. Correlated subqueries are useful for row-wise comparisons and dynamic filtering but are typically slower for large datasets. Non-correlated subqueries are more efficient as they avoid repeated execution. Both are essential tools for writing expressive and powerful SQL queries.

Q.24. Explain the different types of constraints in SQL.

Answer:

Constraints in SQL are rules applied to table columns to maintain the integrity, accuracy, and reliability of the data stored. The NOT NULL constraint ensures that a column cannot contain NULL values, while UNIQUE ensures that all values in a column or a combination of columns are distinct. The PRIMARY KEY constraint combines the properties of UNIQUE and NOT NULL to uniquely identify each record in a table. FOREIGN KEY constraints enforce referential integrity by ensuring that a value in one table matches a primary key in another table, which maintains relationships between tables. The CHECK constraint allows conditions to be specified for values in a column, such as restricting age to values above 18, and the DEFAULT constraint automatically assigns a default value to a column if no value is provided during insertion. These constraints are fundamental to relational databases because they prevent invalid data from entering the system and enforce relationships between entities.

Q.25. Describe aggregate functions in SQL with examples.

Answer:

Aggregate functions in SQL are used to perform calculations on multiple rows of a table and return a single summary value. Common aggregate functions include COUNT(), which counts the number of rows matching a condition, such as SELECT COUNT(*) FROM Employee;, SUM(), which adds up numeric values in a column, for example, SELECT SUM(Salary) FROM Employee;, and AVG(), which computes the average value of a column. Other functions include MAX() and MIN(), which return the highest and lowest values, respectively. Aggregate functions are frequently used with the GROUP BY clause to calculate summaries for groups of rows. For instance, SELECT DeptID, AVG(Salary) FROM Employee GROUP BY DeptID; computes the average salary per department. These functions are essential for reporting and analytics and can also be combined with the HAVING clause to filter groups based on aggregated values, such as finding departments where the average salary exceeds a specified threshold.

Q.26. Differentiate between clustered and non-clustered indexes.

Answer:

A clustered index determines the physical order of data rows in a table. When a clustered index is created, the rows are stored on disk in the same order as the index, and only one clustered index is allowed per table because the data itself can only be ordered in one way. For example, a primary key often creates a clustered index by default. Non-clustered indexes, however, store index data separately from the actual table data and maintain pointers to the rows in the table. A table can have multiple non-clustered indexes. While clustered indexes are faster for range-based queries because of the physical ordering, non-clustered indexes are ideal for queries involving multiple search patterns and for columns that are not part of the primary key. Each type of index enhances query performance but comes with maintenance overhead during insertions, updates, or deletions.

Q.27. What is a transaction? Discuss its properties.

Answer:

A transaction is a sequence of database operations that are treated as a single logical unit of work. Transactions are crucial for maintaining data integrity in multi-user environments and must satisfy four ACID properties. Atomicity ensures that either all operations in a transaction are completed successfully or none are applied, so the database is never left in a partial state. Consistency guarantees that a transaction brings the database from one valid state to another while preserving integrity constraints. Isolation ensures that concurrent transactions do not interfere with each other, making it appear as though transactions are executed serially even if they run simultaneously. Durability means that once a transaction commits, its changes are permanent and will survive system failures. In SQL, transactions are managed using commands like BEGIN TRANSACTION, COMMIT, and ROLLBACK. Together, these properties ensure that databases remain reliable and robust even in high-concurrency environments.

Q.28. Explain concurrency control techniques in DBMS.

Answer:

Concurrency control in DBMS is the set of techniques used to manage simultaneous access to the database by multiple transactions while ensuring data integrity. One widely used technique is locking, where transactions acquire locks on data items before accessing them. Two-phase locking (2PL) is a protocol that requires all locks to be acquired before any are released, ensuring serializability but risking deadlocks. Another approach is timestamp ordering, where transactions are ordered by their timestamps, and operations that violate the order are delayed or rolled back. Optimistic concurrency control allows transactions to proceed without restrictions and validates them only at commit time, which is useful when conflicts are rare. Deadlocks, where two transactions wait indefinitely for each other's locks, are handled by detection (using wait-for graphs) or prevention strategies like wait-die and wound-wait. Concurrency control prevents anomalies such as dirty reads, lost updates, and ensures that database operations are consistent and reliable.

Q.29. Define isolation levels in SQL with examples.

Answer:

Isolation levels in SQL control the visibility of uncommitted changes made by one transaction to others, balancing data consistency and system performance. The four standard isolation levels are Read Uncommitted, Read Committed, Repeatable Read, and Serializable. At Read Uncommitted, transactions may see uncommitted changes from others, allowing dirty reads. Read Committed allows only committed data to be visible, preventing dirty reads but still permitting non-repeatable reads, where a row's value changes between two reads. Repeatable Read prevents dirty and non-repeatable reads by locking rows read, but it can still allow phantom reads—new rows appearing in subsequent queries. Serializable is the strictest level, ensuring full serializability by preventing all anomalies but potentially reducing concurrency. In SQL Server, isolation levels can be set using SET TRANSACTION ISOLATION LEVEL SERIALIZABLE;. Choosing the right level depends on the application: financial systems favor Serializable for accuracy, while reporting systems may use Read Committed for speed.

Q.30. What is deadlock? How is it detected and prevented in DBMS?

Answer:

A deadlock occurs when two or more transactions are waiting indefinitely for resources locked by each other, creating a cycle of dependencies. For example, Transaction A holds a lock on Resource X and waits for Resource Y, while Transaction B holds a lock on Resource Y and waits for Resource X. Deadlocks are detected in DBMS by constructing a wait-for graph, where transactions are nodes and edges represent waiting relationships; a cycle in the graph indicates a deadlock. To resolve it, the system can abort one or more transactions involved in the cycle. Deadlocks can also be prevented proactively using techniques such as lock ordering, where transactions request locks in a predefined sequence to avoid cycles, or timeout mechanisms, where transactions are aborted if they wait too long. Other prevention strategies include the wait-die and wound-wait schemes, which use transaction timestamps to decide which transaction waits and which is rolled back. Proper deadlock handling ensures system stability and fair access in multi-user environments.

Q.31. What is the difference between logical and physical data independence?

Answer: Logical and physical data independence are two critical concepts in database design that allow changes to be made at one level of abstraction without affecting other levels. Logical data independence refers to the capacity to change the logical schema such as adding new tables, attributes, or relationships without requiring modifications to the external schemas or application programs. For instance, adding a new "Email" field to a Student table should not require rewriting queries that only use the existing fields. Logical independence is challenging to achieve because application programs are often tightly coupled with specific table structures. On the other hand, physical data independence refers to the ability to change the physical storage or access methods without altering the conceptual schema. For example, reorganizing a table's storage from heap file organization to B+ tree indexing should not affect queries or application logic. Physical independence is easier to maintain because such changes are typically invisible to users and applications. Together, these two forms of independence enable flexible, maintainable systems by isolating applications from underlying data storage details and schema evolution.

Q.32. Explain the concept of a materialized view in databases.

Answer: A materialized view is a database object that stores the results of a query physically, unlike a regular view that acts as a virtual table and recalculates results on each access. Materialized views are particularly useful in scenarios where queries are complex and involve multiple joins, aggregations, or computations that are expensive to execute repeatedly. For example, in a sales data warehouse, a materialized view could precompute total sales per region for faster reporting. Because the data is stored, materialized views need mechanisms to refresh their content to reflect changes in the base tables. Refresh strategies include on-demand refresh, where updates occur manually or when explicitly triggered, and incremental refresh, where only the changes since the last update are applied. While materialized views improve query performance and support high-volume analytics, they come with storage overhead and maintenance costs. Choosing when to use them involves trade-offs between query speed, freshness of data, and system resources.

Q.33. Describe the Two-Phase Commit Protocol in distributed databases.

Answer: The Two-Phase Commit (2PC) protocol is a distributed algorithm used to ensure atomicity in transactions spanning multiple database systems. It involves two distinct phases: the prepare phase and the commit phase. In the prepare phase, the coordinator sends a "prepare to commit" message to all participating sites, asking them to vote on whether they are ready to commit. Each participant performs necessary local operations, writes data to a log, and responds with a "ready" or "abort" vote. If all participants vote "ready," the protocol moves to the commit phase, where the coordinator sends a "commit" message, and each site makes the changes permanent. If any site votes to abort, the coordinator sends a "rollback" message, undoing all changes. 2PC ensures that either all systems commit the transaction or none do, maintaining consistency across distributed systems. However, it is vulnerable to blocking if the coordinator crashes during the commit phase, and variants like Three-Phase Commit attempt to mitigate this.

Q.34. Explain the difference between OLTP and OLAP systems.

Answer: OLTP (Online Transaction Processing) and OLAP (Online Analytical Processing) are two distinct types of database systems designed for different purposes. OLTP systems are optimized for handling a large number of short, atomic transactions like inserting, updating, or deleting records. They are used in operational systems such as banking, e-commerce, and reservations, where speed, accuracy, and concurrency control are crucial. OLAP systems, on the other hand, are designed for complex queries and analysis of large volumes of historical data. They support multidimensional data models, aggregations, and trend analysis, making them ideal for decision support and business intelligence applications. OLTP databases are normalized to avoid redundancy and maintain data integrity, whereas OLAP databases are often denormalized or structured into star and snowflake schemas to optimize read-heavy operations. While OLTP prioritizes transaction throughput and response time, OLAP focuses on query performance and flexibility for analytical reporting.

Q.35. What is the difference between star schema and snowflake schema?

Answer: The star schema and snowflake schema are two common data modeling approaches used in data warehousing. In a star schema, there is a central fact table containing quantitative data (such as sales amount or quantity) surrounded by denormalized dimension tables (such as Customer, Product, and Time) directly linked to the fact table. This design simplifies queries and enhances performance by reducing the number of joins needed. In contrast, a snowflake schema normalizes dimension tables, breaking them into multiple related tables to remove redundancy. For example, in a snowflake schema, the "Location" information might be split into separate tables for City, State, and Country, each linked hierarchically. While snowflake schemas save storage and improve data integrity, they require more complex queries with multiple joins, which can affect performance. Star schemas are preferred for simplicity and speed in OLAP systems, while snowflake schemas are chosen when space efficiency and strict normalization are priorities.

Q.36. Explain indexing and its types in detail.

Answer: Indexing in databases is a technique used to speed up data retrieval operations by creating a data structure that allows quick access to rows in a table based on key values. Without indexes, a DBMS would need to scan entire tables for queries, which is inefficient for large datasets. There are various types of indexes: Primary indexes are automatically created on the primary key and enforce uniqueness, while secondary indexes are created on non-key columns to optimize queries. Clustered indexes determine the physical order of data rows in a table, making range-based queries fast but limiting a table to a single clustered index. Non-clustered indexes create a separate structure with pointers to actual rows, allowing multiple indexes per table but requiring extra lookups. Composite indexes involve multiple columns to optimize multi-column searches. Bitmap indexes, used in data warehouses, represent data compactly for columns with low cardinality. Proper indexing balances read performance against increased storage use and slower write operations due to index maintenance.

Q.37. What is query optimization in DBMS? Why is it important?

Answer: Query optimization is the process by which a DBMS evaluates multiple strategies to execute a query and selects the one with the lowest estimated cost in terms of CPU, memory, and I/O operations. When a query is submitted, the query processor generates a parse tree and logical plan. The optimizer applies transformation rules to rewrite the query (such as pushing selections closer to base tables) and considers different access paths like index scans or table scans. It estimates the cost of each physical plan based on statistics such as table size and index selectivity. The chosen plan is then executed by the DBMS. Optimization is critical because the difference between the best and worst plan can be orders of magnitude in execution time, especially for large datasets or complex joins. Poorly optimized queries can lead to bottlenecks, high latency, and resource exhaustion. Advanced systems support both rule-based and cost-based optimization to achieve efficient query execution.

Q.38. Describe the concept of hashing in databases.

Answer: Hashing is a technique used in databases to map data to a fixed-size address space for efficient access. It involves applying a hash function to a key attribute to compute a hash value that determines where a record is stored or retrieved. In static hashing, the hash table has a fixed size, and collisions (where two keys produce the same hash value) are resolved using techniques like chaining (linked lists) or open addressing (probing for alternate slots). Dynamic hashing, such as extendible or linear hashing, allows the hash table to grow or shrink dynamically as data volume changes, avoiding overflow issues common in static hashing. Hashing is particularly efficient for equality searches because it provides near-constant access time, unlike index-based access which depends on tree traversal. However, it is unsuitable for range queries because keys are not ordered. Hashing is widely used in hash indexes, distributed databases for partitioning data, and in-memory caches for fast key-value lookups.

Q.39. What is a surrogate key? When is it used?

Answer: A surrogate key is an artificial key assigned to uniquely identify rows in a table, often implemented as an auto-incremented integer or a globally unique identifier (GUID). Unlike natural keys, which use existing business data like Social Security Numbers or email addresses, surrogate keys have no inherent meaning to users and exist solely for technical purposes. Surrogate keys are commonly used when no suitable natural key exists or when natural keys are composite, large, or prone to changes, which can lead to referential integrity issues. For example, in a Customer table, using a CustomerID as a surrogate key avoids problems if a customer's email (a potential natural key) changes. They are also useful in data warehouses to handle slowly changing dimensions where historical tracking requires stable identifiers. The main drawback of surrogate keys is that they add another layer of abstraction, requiring additional joins to fetch meaningful attributes.

Q.40. Explain the difference between procedural and declarative query languages.

Answer: Procedural query languages require the user to specify both what data to retrieve and how to retrieve it, outlining the step-by-step process. Relational algebra is a procedural language where operations like selection, projection, and join must be explicitly defined. Declarative query languages, such as SQL, allow users to specify what data they want without detailing the retrieval process; the DBMS determines the optimal execution strategy. For example, SELECT Name FROM Employee WHERE DeptID = 5; specifies the desired result, leaving the DBMS to choose between scanning the table or using an index. Procedural languages provide more control and can be useful for optimization in certain contexts, but they require detailed knowledge of the database structure. Declarative languages are user-friendly, promote logical abstraction, and are preferred in modern relational systems because they enable the DBMS to apply sophisticated query optimization techniques.

Chapter 5: Most Asked Important Questions Part-B

Q.41. What are ACID properties in DBMS? Explain with examples.

Answer: ACID is an acronym for Atomicity, Consistency, Isolation, and Durability four essential properties that ensure reliable transaction processing in a DBMS. Atomicity guarantees that a transaction is treated as an indivisible unit of work; either all operations are completed successfully, or none are applied. For example, in a funds transfer between two accounts, both debit and credit operations must succeed together or rollback entirely. Consistency ensures that a transaction transforms the database from one valid state to another while maintaining defined integrity constraints. If a constraint like "balance ≥ 0" exists, transactions cannot leave the database in an invalid state. Isolation means that concurrent transactions execute as if they were serial, so intermediate results of one transaction are not visible to others. Without proper isolation, phenomena like dirty reads or lost updates can occur. Finally, Durability ensures that once a transaction commits, its effects persist even if the system crashes afterward. To enforce durability, DBMSs use mechanisms like write-ahead logging. Together, ACID properties maintain data correctness and integrity, even under high concurrency and system failures.

Q.42. Discuss the concept of shadow paging for recovery in DBMS.

Answer: Shadow paging is a recovery technique in DBMS that maintains database consistency without requiring complex logs. It involves creating a copy (or shadow) of the database's page table at the start of a transaction. The system maintains two page tables: the current page table, which reflects uncommitted changes, and the shadow page table, which points to the original, stable pages. All modifications during the transaction are performed on copies of the data pages, leaving the shadow pages untouched. When the transaction commits, the DBMS atomically switches the pointer from the shadow page table to the current one, making the changes permanent. If the transaction aborts or the system crashes before commit, the shadow page table is retained, effectively discarding uncommitted changes. Shadow paging avoids redo and undo operations and provides atomicity and durability with minimal overhead. However, it requires additional storage and can be inefficient for large transactions due to frequent copying and pointer management.

Q.43. Explain the role of checkpoints in database recovery.

Answer: Checkpoints are a mechanism in DBMS recovery that helps reduce the amount of work required after a system crash. A checkpoint is a point in time when the DBMS ensures that all modifications in memory buffers are written to the physical database on disk, and the transaction log is synchronized. During normal operations, a DBMS keeps many changes in memory to improve performance. If the system crashes, it must replay the log to redo committed transactions and undo incomplete ones. By setting a checkpoint, the DBMS creates a safe state from which recovery can begin, ignoring earlier log entries because the database is already consistent up to that point. Checkpoints can be fuzzy, allowing transactions to continue during the checkpoint, or quiescent, where transactions are temporarily suspended. They significantly reduce recovery time by limiting the log scan range and are essential in large-scale systems where transactions generate high volumes of log records.

Q.44. What are the differences between primary key, candidate key, and foreign key?

Answer: A primary key is a column or combination of columns that uniquely identifies each row in a table and cannot contain NULL values. Only one primary key is allowed per table, and it enforces entity integrity. A candidate key is any attribute set that uniquely identifies rows in a table; there may be multiple candidate keys in a table, but one is chosen as the primary key while the others are known as alternate keys. For example, in a Student table, RollNo and Email may both uniquely identify students, making them candidate keys, but only RollNo may be selected as the primary key. A foreign key, on the other hand, is an attribute in one table that references the primary key in another table to establish and enforce a link between related data. For example, in an Enrollment table, StudentID can be a foreign key referencing Student.RollNo. Foreign keys maintain referential integrity between tables, ensuring that no orphaned records exist.

Q.45. Describe the difference between DELETE, TRUNCATE, and DROP commands in SQL.

Answer: The DELETE, TRUNCATE, and DROP commands in SQL are used to remove data, but they differ in scope and behavior. The DELETE command removes rows from a table based on an optional WHERE clause, allowing selective deletion. For example, DELETE FROM Employee WHERE DeptID = 5; removes only employees in department 5. DELETE operations are logged for each row deleted, and they can be rolled back if wrapped in a transaction. The TRUNCATE command removes all rows from a table instantly without logging individual row deletions. Unlike DELETE, TRUNCATE cannot include a WHERE clause and is faster because it deallocates the entire data pages. However, TRUNCATE may also reset identity columns and is less flexible. The DROP command deletes an entire table, including its structure, constraints, indexes, and data, making it unrecoverable unless the table is recreated. For example, DROP TABLE Employee; removes the Employee table from the database entirely. DELETE and TRUNCATE operate on data, while DROP affects the schema itself.

Q.46. What is a stored procedure? How does it differ from a trigger?

Answer: A stored procedure is a precompiled set of SQL statements and optional procedural logic stored in the database and executed on demand. It can accept input parameters, return output values, and encapsulate complex operations such as validating data, performing calculations, or executing multiple SQL queries as a unit. For example, a stored procedure TransferFunds(@FromAccount, @ToAccount, @Amount) might handle debiting and crediting accounts in a single transaction. In contrast, a trigger is a special type of stored program that automatically executes in response to specific events on a table, such as INSERT, UPDATE, or DELETE operations. Unlike stored procedures, triggers are invoked implicitly and cannot be called directly by users or applications. Triggers are typically used to enforce business rules, maintain audit trails, or synchronize related tables. Stored procedures provide explicit, reusable logic that must be invoked manually, whereas triggers enforce automatic, reactive behavior tied to data modifications.

Q.47. Explain the differences between horizontal and vertical fragmentation in distributed databases.

Answer: In distributed databases, fragmentation divides tables into smaller pieces for storage across multiple sites to improve performance and availability. Horizontal fragmentation partitions a table into subsets of rows based on certain criteria. For example, an Employee table might be split such that employees in the “North” region are stored at one site and those in the “South” region at another. Queries accessing only regional data benefit from reduced transmission and faster response. Vertical fragmentation, on the other hand, divides a table into subsets of columns. For instance, sensitive columns like Salary and SSN may be stored separately from general information such as Name and Department. Each fragment must include the primary key to allow reconstruction through joins. Horizontal fragmentation optimizes access by location, while vertical fragmentation optimizes for access by attributes. Both types support localized queries, but vertical fragmentation often requires more joins to reassemble data.

Q.48. What are multivalued dependencies and how do they relate to 4NF?

Answer: A multivalued dependency (MVD) in a relation exists when, for a given value of attribute A, there are multiple independent values of attribute B, and this dependency is not a functional dependency. For example, consider a table with attributes Student, Hobby, and Language. A student can have multiple hobbies and multiple languages, and these sets are independent of each other. This redundancy can cause anomalies during updates or deletions. A relation is in Fourth Normal Form (4NF) if it is in Boyce-Codd Normal Form (BCNF) and has no non-trivial multivalued dependencies other than a candidate key. To remove MVDs and achieve 4NF, the table is decomposed into separate relations for each multivalued dependency, such as Student-Hobby and Student-Language tables. This decomposition ensures data independence and eliminates redundancy while maintaining lossless joins.

Q.49. Describe object-relational databases and their features.

Answer: Object-relational databases (ORDBMS) extend traditional relational databases by integrating features of object-oriented programming. They allow storage of complex data types such as multimedia, geospatial data, and user-defined objects alongside traditional tables. ORDBMSs support concepts like inheritance, polymorphism, and encapsulation. For example, a Vehicle class can have subtypes Car and Bike, allowing a single table to store diverse but related entities. ORDBMSs also permit user-defined types and functions, enabling operations directly on complex objects. Features like table inheritance and object identifiers enhance flexibility for modern applications such as computer-aided design (CAD), scientific databases, and multimedia repositories. Unlike pure object-oriented databases, ORDBMSs maintain compatibility with SQL, making them suitable for systems transitioning from relational to object-oriented paradigms.

Q.50. What is a data warehouse and how does it differ from a database?

Answer: A data warehouse is a centralized repository designed for storing large volumes of historical and current data from multiple heterogeneous sources for analytical and reporting purposes. Unlike operational databases optimized for transactional processing (OLTP), data warehouses are structured for Online Analytical Processing (OLAP), supporting complex queries, aggregations, and trend analysis. Data warehouses use ETL (Extract, Transform, Load) processes to collect, clean, and integrate data into a unified schema. They typically employ multidimensional models such as star or snowflake schemas to facilitate fast analysis across dimensions like time, geography, or product lines. While databases prioritize concurrency, normalization, and transaction speed, data warehouses prioritize query performance, denormalization, and historical data storage. Businesses use data warehouses for decision support, forecasting, and performance monitoring.

Q.51. Explain the concept of data mining and its applications in database systems.

Answer: Data mining is the process of discovering hidden patterns, correlations, and useful information from large datasets using statistical, mathematical, and machine learning techniques. It goes beyond simple data querying by identifying trends and relationships that are not immediately obvious. In the context of database systems, data mining enables organizations to analyze historical data stored in warehouses and extract actionable insights for decision-making. Common techniques include classification, which assigns records to predefined categories; clustering, which groups similar records without predefined labels; association rule mining, which finds relationships between variables (e.g., "customers who buy bread often buy butter"); and anomaly detection, which identifies unusual patterns that may indicate fraud or errors. Applications of data mining span multiple domains: in retail, it is used for market basket analysis and customer segmentation; in healthcare, for predicting disease outbreaks and personalizing treatment plans; in finance, for credit scoring and fraud detection. Data mining transforms static data repositories into dynamic knowledge sources, making it a cornerstone of business intelligence and predictive analytics.

Q.52. Differentiate between operational databases and data warehouses.

Answer: Operational databases and data warehouses serve distinct purposes within an organization's data ecosystem. Operational databases are designed to support day-to-day business processes and transactions. They handle frequent inserts, updates, and deletes and are optimized for speed and concurrency in Online Transaction Processing (OLTP) systems. These databases are highly normalized to reduce redundancy and ensure data integrity. In contrast, data warehouses are designed for analytical purposes and decision support. They store historical data consolidated from multiple sources and are optimized for complex queries, aggregations, and reporting in Online Analytical Processing (OLAP) systems. Data warehouses typically use denormalized schemas like star or snowflake to improve query performance and support multidimensional analysis. While operational databases focus on the current state of business operations, data warehouses provide a historical perspective, enabling organizations to identify trends, perform forecasting, and make strategic decisions.

Q.53. What are distributed databases? Explain their advantages and disadvantages.

Answer: A distributed database is a collection of multiple logically interrelated databases distributed across different physical locations but connected via a network. Each site in a distributed database system manages its local data and can process queries independently or in collaboration with other sites. The main advantages include improved reliability and availability, as the failure of one site does not render the entire system unusable; scalability, since data and workload can be distributed across multiple servers; and localization of data access, which improves performance for geographically dispersed users. However, distributed databases also come with disadvantages such as increased complexity in managing data consistency across sites, higher overhead due to synchronization, and potential security challenges over networks. Ensuring atomicity and isolation of transactions across distributed nodes requires sophisticated protocols like Two-Phase Commit (2PC) and concurrency control mechanisms. Despite these challenges, distributed databases are essential in global applications like banking, telecommunications, and e-commerce.

Q.54. Explain the differences between horizontal and vertical scaling in database systems.

Answer: Horizontal and vertical scaling are two approaches to improve database performance and handle increased workloads. Horizontal scaling, also known as scaling out, involves adding more servers or nodes to distribute data and processing across multiple machines. This approach is commonly used in distributed systems and cloud environments, where databases like MongoDB or Cassandra partition data across nodes. Horizontal scaling provides better fault tolerance and virtually unlimited growth potential but requires complex coordination mechanisms such as sharding and load balancing. Vertical scaling, or scaling up, enhances the capacity of a single server by adding more CPU, memory, or storage. Relational databases like Oracle or SQL Server often rely on vertical scaling for performance improvements. While vertical scaling is simpler and requires fewer architectural changes, it has physical limits and can become costly as hardware requirements increase. Modern architectures often combine both approaches to achieve optimal performance and resilience.

Q.55. What is the role of middleware in distributed databases?

Answer: Middleware in distributed databases acts as an intermediary layer that facilitates communication and coordination between client applications and distributed database servers. It abstracts the complexities of managing distributed data and presents a unified interface to users. Middleware is responsible for query decomposition, ensuring that a global query is broken into sub-queries executable on different sites and then recombining results seamlessly. It handles transaction management using protocols like Two-Phase Commit to maintain atomicity and consistency across multiple nodes. Additionally, middleware provides load balancing by directing queries to appropriate servers based on current workloads and supports replication and synchronization to ensure data consistency. It can also implement security measures such as authentication and encryption in distributed environments. By insulating clients from the underlying distributed architecture, middleware simplifies application development and improves scalability and reliability in systems like cloud databases and enterprise data warehouses.

Q.56. What are the advantages of using NoSQL databases over traditional RDBMS?

Answer: NoSQL databases offer advantages over traditional relational databases, especially in handling large-scale, unstructured, or semi-structured data. One major advantage is their schema flexibility; unlike RDBMS, which requires predefined schemas, NoSQL databases can store diverse data formats such as JSON, XML, or key-value pairs without rigid structures. This makes them ideal for rapidly evolving applications. NoSQL databases are also designed for horizontal scalability, allowing them to distribute data across multiple nodes seamlessly, which is crucial for web-scale applications and big data systems. They support high throughput for read and write operations, making them suitable for workloads like real-time analytics, IoT data, and social media feeds. Additionally, some NoSQL systems like Cassandra or MongoDB provide built-in replication and fault tolerance, ensuring high availability. However, NoSQL databases often trade off consistency (as in the CAP theorem) for availability and partition tolerance, adopting eventual consistency models instead of strong ACID guarantees.

Q.57. Explain the CAP theorem in the context of distributed databases.

Answer: The CAP theorem, proposed by Eric Brewer, states that in a distributed system, it is impossible to simultaneously guarantee all three properties: Consistency, Availability, and Partition tolerance. Consistency ensures that all nodes in the system reflect the same data at any given time. Availability means that every request receives a response, even if some nodes have failed. Partition tolerance ensures that the system continues to operate despite network partitions or failures that split nodes into disjoint subsets. In practice, distributed databases must choose between consistency and availability when partition tolerance is inevitable due to network unreliability. For instance, traditional RDBMS prioritize consistency over availability, while NoSQL databases like Cassandra and DynamoDB often favor availability and partition tolerance, adopting eventual consistency models. The CAP theorem guides architects in making trade-offs based on application requirements, such as favoring consistency in financial systems or availability in social media platforms.

Q.58. Describe the differences between centralized and distributed DBMS.

Answer: A centralized DBMS manages data stored in a single location and accessed by clients over a network. It offers simplicity in administration, data consistency, and security but can suffer from performance bottlenecks and a single point of failure. In contrast, a distributed DBMS stores and manages data across multiple sites connected via a network, presenting a unified database view to users. Distributed DBMSs improve availability, fault tolerance, and scalability by replicating or partitioning data across nodes. However, they introduce complexities in ensuring data consistency, managing distributed transactions, and handling network failures. Centralized DBMSs are suitable for smaller, localized applications, whereas distributed DBMSs are essential for global organizations requiring high availability and access from multiple geographic regions.

Q.59. What are triggers in SQL? Discuss their types and uses.

Answer: A trigger in SQL is a procedural code that automatically executes in response to specific events on a table or view, such as INSERT, UPDATE, or DELETE operations. Triggers are used to enforce business rules, maintain audit trails, or propagate changes across related tables. They are classified into BEFORE triggers, which execute before the triggering statement and can modify or validate incoming data, and AFTER triggers, which execute after the statement completes, suitable for logging and notifications. Some systems also support INSTEAD OF triggers to override standard operations, particularly useful for views. For example, a BEFORE INSERT trigger on an Employee table might validate that salary values are within a specified range, while an AFTER UPDATE trigger could log changes to a history table. Triggers provide automatic, consistent enforcement of constraints but can add complexity and should be designed carefully to avoid performance issues and unintended side effects.

Q.60. Explain the concept of query decomposition in distributed DBMS.

Answer: Query decomposition in distributed DBMS is the process of breaking down a global query into smaller sub-queries that can be executed on local databases at different sites. This process begins with query parsing and validation, where the global query is analyzed for syntax and semantic correctness. Next, the query is rewritten into an equivalent form that optimizes execution, such as pushing selections and projections closer to base tables to reduce intermediate result sizes. The query is then fragmented, assigning each part to the site where the relevant data resides. The final step is assembly, where results from local queries are combined to produce the final global result. Query decomposition ensures efficient execution by leveraging parallelism and minimizing data transfer across the network. It also helps maintain transparency for users, who perceive the distributed database as a single logical unit despite its physical distribution.

Q.71. What is the difference between procedural and non-procedural query languages with examples?

Answer: Procedural and non-procedural query languages differ in how they allow users to interact with the database. Procedural query languages require the user to specify both what data is needed and how to retrieve it. They describe a sequence of operations that the DBMS should perform to fetch the result. Relational algebra is an example of a procedural language, where operations like selection, projection, and joins are explicitly defined. For instance, retrieving names of employees in a particular department involves defining the sequence: first perform a selection on the DepartmentID, then a projection on the Name column. In contrast, non-procedural query languages require the user to specify only what data is needed without specifying the retrieval strategy. SQL is a non-procedural language; for example, SELECT Name FROM Employee WHERE DeptID=5; asks for names of employees in department 5 without dictating the execution plan. Non-procedural languages abstract the retrieval process, allowing the DBMS to optimize queries automatically, making them more user-friendly and efficient for most applications.

Q.72. Explain the concept of serializability in DBMS with an example.

Answer: Serializability is a concept in DBMS used to ensure that concurrent transactions produce the same effect as if the transactions were executed serially, one after another. It is a key criterion for correctness in concurrent transaction execution. Consider two transactions: T1 transfers funds from Account A to Account B, and T2 applies interest to both accounts. If executed concurrently without control, the operations might interleave in a way that results in lost updates or inconsistencies. Serializability ensures that such interleaved execution is equivalent to some serial execution order, preserving database consistency. The DBMS uses techniques like locking and timestamp ordering to enforce serializability. There are two main types: conflict serializability, where conflicting operations (reads and writes on the same data) are scheduled to avoid interference, and view serializability, which considers the overall read/write patterns. Enforcing serializability prevents anomalies like dirty reads, non-repeatable reads, and phantom rows in multi-user environments.

Q.73. What are phantom reads in DBMS? How are they prevented?

Answer: A phantom read occurs in a database when a transaction executes the same query multiple times and retrieves different results because another concurrent transaction has inserted or deleted rows matching the query's condition. For example, Transaction T1 reads all employees in department 10. While T1 is active, Transaction T2 inserts a new employee into department 10. If T1 re-executes the query, it now sees an additional row that wasn't there before, creating a phantom read. Phantom reads violate isolation by allowing the data set visible to a transaction to change unexpectedly. To prevent this, DBMSs use higher isolation levels like Serializable, which ensures transactions operate as if executed serially. Serializable isolation achieves this by locking entire ranges of rows or tables, preventing other transactions from inserting or deleting rows that could create phantoms. Alternatively, predicate locks or index-range locks are used to lock data sets defined by query predicates rather than individual rows.

Q.74. Differentiate between eager and lazy evaluation in query processing.

Answer: Eager and lazy evaluation are two strategies used in query processing to execute operations and produce results. In eager evaluation, operations are executed as soon as they are encountered, and intermediate results are materialized (stored) for subsequent operations. For example, in a query involving joins and filters, the DBMS might compute and store the join result immediately before applying filters. This approach is simple and can be efficient if intermediate results are reused multiple times, but it may consume significant memory and I/O resources if the intermediate data sets are large. In contrast, lazy evaluation (also known as pipelining) delays computation until results are actually needed, passing rows from one operation to the next on demand. For instance, instead of materializing the join result, rows are fetched and filtered incrementally. Lazy evaluation reduces memory usage and avoids unnecessary computations when only a subset of results is required. However, it may be less efficient for queries that need the entire result set. Modern DBMSs often combine both strategies for optimal performance.

Q.75. What is query rewriting in DBMS? Give an example.

Answer: Query rewriting in DBMS is a process where the system transforms a user's query into an equivalent form that is more efficient to execute while returning the same result. It is part of the query optimization phase and uses equivalence rules to modify the query structure. For example, consider the query SELECT * FROM Employee WHERE DeptID IN (SELECT DeptID FROM Department WHERE Location='Delhi');. The DBMS might rewrite this using a join: SELECT E.* FROM Employee E INNER JOIN Department D ON E.DeptID = D.DeptID WHERE D.Location='Delhi';. This rewritten query allows the optimizer to use join algorithms and indexes more effectively, potentially reducing execution time. Query rewriting can also involve techniques like predicate pushdown, where filtering conditions are applied as early as possible in the query plan to minimize intermediate data, and subquery unnesting, where nested queries are converted to joins. These transformations enhance performance without altering the semantic meaning of the query.

Q.76. Explain the concept of replication in distributed databases.

Answer: Replication in distributed databases is the process of storing copies of the same data at multiple sites to improve availability, fault tolerance, and performance. When data is replicated, users can access the nearest copy, reducing latency and ensuring system resilience even if one site fails. Replication can be synchronous, where updates are propagated to all replicas simultaneously before committing, ensuring strong consistency but introducing higher latency. Alternatively, it can be asynchronous, where updates are propagated after the local commit, allowing faster response times but risking temporary inconsistencies (eventual consistency). Replication strategies include full replication, where the entire database is copied at all sites, and partial replication, where only subsets of data are replicated based on access patterns. While replication improves reliability, it introduces challenges in maintaining consistency across replicas, especially during concurrent updates. Techniques like conflict resolution, versioning, and quorum-based protocols help manage these issues in modern distributed systems.

Q.77. What is a transaction log and how is it used for recovery?

Answer: A transaction log is a sequential record maintained by a DBMS to track all changes made to the database. Each log entry typically contains information about the transaction ID, operation performed (INSERT, UPDATE, DELETE), affected data items, and before-and-after values. The log plays a crucial role in ensuring atomicity and durability during failures. For recovery, the DBMS uses the log in two main ways: redo and undo. If the system crashes, committed transactions are redone by replaying their operations from the log, ensuring their effects persist. Uncommitted transactions are undone by reversing their operations using the before-images in the log. The write-ahead logging (WAL) protocol enforces that log entries are written to stable storage before the corresponding data changes are applied to the database, guaranteeing recoverability. Transaction logs enable DBMSs to recover to a consistent state after crashes and are the foundation for features like point-in-time recovery and replication.

Q.78. Explain the difference between eager and lazy replication.

Answer: Eager and lazy replication are two strategies used to maintain consistency in replicated databases. In eager replication, updates to a replicated data item are applied to all copies simultaneously as part of the same transaction. This approach ensures strong consistency, as all replicas reflect the same state immediately after the transaction commits. However, eager replication can be costly in terms of communication overhead and transaction latency, especially in geographically distributed systems. Lazy replication, on the other hand, allows updates to be applied to one replica first, with changes propagated to other replicas asynchronously. This reduces response time for the client and improves system availability, but it can result in temporary inconsistencies where some replicas are stale until synchronization completes. Lazy replication is suitable for applications tolerant of eventual consistency, such as caching systems or social media feeds

Q.79. What is the difference between centralized and decentralized concurrency control?

Answer: Centralized and decentralized concurrency control are two approaches for managing concurrent transactions in distributed database systems. In centralized concurrency control, a single site is responsible for coordinating all transactions and enforcing serializability. It simplifies conflict resolution and maintains global consistency but creates a bottleneck and single point of failure. For example, all lock requests are handled by a central lock manager. In contrast, decentralized concurrency control distributes the responsibility across multiple sites, with each site managing its local data and coordinating with others as needed. Protocols like distributed two-phase locking or timestamp ordering are used to ensure global serializability. Decentralized control improves system scalability and fault tolerance but requires complex mechanisms for detecting and resolving conflicts across sites.

Q.80. Describe optimistic concurrency control and its use cases.

Answer: Optimistic concurrency control (OCC) is a technique used in DBMS to manage concurrent transactions without using locks during the execution phase. OCC assumes that conflicts between transactions are rare, so it allows transactions to proceed without restrictions and checks for conflicts only at commit time. Each transaction undergoes three phases: read, where it executes operations and stores tentative changes; validation, where the system checks if the transaction's read and write sets conflict with other concurrent transactions; and write, where changes are applied to the database if validation succeeds, or discarded otherwise.

Printed at Repro India Ltd.